Personal Branding: Building Your Professional Identity Online

Roy Hendershot

Published by Roy Hendershot, 2024.

While every precaution has been taken in the preparation of this book, the publisher assumes no responsibility for errors or omissions, or for damages resulting from the use of the information contained herein.

PERSONAL BRANDING: BUILDING YOUR PROFESSIONAL IDENTITY ONLINE

First edition. June 23, 2024.

Copyright © 2024 Roy Hendershot.

Written by Roy Hendershot.

Table of Contents

Introduction: The Power of Personal Branding 1

Chapter 1: Discovering Your Unique Identity 7

Chapter 2: Crafting Your Personal Brand Story 13

Chapter 3: Building Your Online Presence 19

Chapter 4: Content Creation for Personal Branding 25

Chapter 5: Social Media Strategies for Personal Branding 31

Chapter 6: Networking and Relationship Building 36

Chapter 7: Managing Your Online Reputation 41

Chapter 8: Leveraging Technology and Tools 46

Chapter 9: Monetizing Your Personal Brand 51

Chapter 10: Continuous Improvement and Growth 57

Introduction: The Power of Personal Branding

Personal branding is like crafting your superhero identity. It's about defining who you are, what you stand for, and how you want to be seen by the world. It's not just about being famous; it's about being known for something meaningful and valuable. Imagine you're a superhero; what would your powers be? What kind of costume would you wear? Personal branding is about answering these questions in a way that makes people remember and respect you.

The impact of a strong personal brand can't be overstated. Think about some of the most influential people you know. They didn't just become famous overnight. They worked on building a brand that people could recognize and trust. Whether it's in business, art, or any other field, a powerful personal brand opens doors, creates opportunities, and builds connections. It's like having a magic key that unlocks various possibilities in your career and life.

In the digital age, personal branding has taken on a whole new dimension. With the internet, social media, and digital platforms, your reach is limitless. You can connect with people across the globe, share your ideas, and build a following. This global stage means you need to be more strategic and thoughtful about your personal brand. Every tweet, post, or video contributes to how people perceive you. Your digital footprint is as crucial as your physical presence.

Success stories of personal branding abound. Look at Oprah Winfrey, Elon Musk, or even niche influencers who have carved out a name for themselves in specific fields. These individuals didn't just rely on their skills or luck. They meticulously crafted their personal brands. They knew their strengths, stayed true to their values, and consistently communicated their message. Their stories show that with dedication and the right strategy, anyone can build a compelling personal brand.

Setting goals for your personal brand is essential. Without clear objectives, it's like setting out on a journey without a map. What do you want to achieve with your brand? Do you want to become a thought leader in your industry? Or perhaps you want to create a supportive community around a cause you care about? Whatever your goals, defining them helps you stay focused and measure your progress.

Building confidence in your brand starts with believing in yourself. Self-doubt can be a significant barrier, but remember, even the most successful people had to start somewhere. Embrace your uniqueness and trust that you have something valuable to offer. Confidence is contagious. When you believe in your brand, others will too. It's about projecting a positive image and backing it up with genuine skills and integrity.

Authenticity is the cornerstone of personal branding. In a world full of noise, being genuine makes you stand out. People can spot a fake from miles away, and authenticity builds trust. Don't try to be someone you're not. Embrace your quirks, share your real stories, and let your true self shine. Authenticity attracts people who resonate with you and your values, creating a loyal and engaged audience.

Crafting your brand's message is like writing your personal manifesto. What do you want to say to the world? What are your core values and beliefs? Your message should be clear, concise, and consistent across all platforms. Whether it's your social media bio, your website, or your business card, your message should reflect who you are and what you stand for. A strong, consistent message helps people understand and remember you.

Identifying your target audience is crucial. You can't be everything to everyone, so focus on who you want to reach. Who are the people that will benefit from your message or services? What are their needs and interests? Understanding your audience helps you tailor your content and approach, making your brand more relevant and engaging. It's like speaking directly to the people who matter most to your brand's success.

Building a personal brand strategy is your blueprint for success. It involves setting clear goals, identifying your audience, crafting your message, and planning how to communicate it. Your strategy should also include metrics for measuring success and adjusting your approach as needed. A well-thought-out strategy keeps you on track and ensures that all your branding efforts are aligned and effective.

The role of social media in personal branding can't be ignored. Platforms like Twitter, LinkedIn, and Instagram are powerful tools for building and promoting your brand. They allow you to share your message, connect with your audience, and showcase your expertise. Social media is also a great way to stay current with industry trends and engage in conversations that matter to your brand. It's about being active and present where your audience is.

Networking is another critical aspect of personal branding. Building relationships with other professionals, influencers, and thought leaders can amplify your brand's reach and credibility. Networking isn't just about collecting business cards; it's about forming meaningful connections that can lead to collaborations, opportunities, and support. It's about being part of a community that shares and promotes each other's growth.

Maintaining consistency in your brand is vital. Your message, visuals, and tone should be uniform across all platforms and communications. Consistency helps reinforce your brand and makes it more recognizable. Whether it's the colors you use, the style of your posts, or the way you interact with your audience, consistency builds trust and familiarity.

Adapting your brand over time is necessary. As you grow and evolve, so should your brand. Staying static can make you seem outdated or out of touch. Be open to change, learn from feedback, and be willing to adjust your strategy to stay relevant. Adapting doesn't mean losing your core values but rather finding new ways to express them in a changing landscape.

The benefits of a strong personal brand are manifold. It opens doors to new opportunities, builds your credibility, and can even lead to financial gains. A strong brand makes you a magnet for opportunities, whether it's a new job, a speaking gig, or a partnership. It also gives you a platform to share your message and make a positive impact.

Challenges in personal branding are inevitable. From dealing with negative feedback to staying motivated, building a personal brand requires resilience and perseverance. It's not always a smooth ride, but the rewards are worth the effort. Understanding potential challenges and having strategies to overcome them can keep you on the path to success.

Measuring the success of your personal brand involves looking at various metrics. These can include social media engagement, website traffic, and professional opportunities that come your way. Regularly reviewing these metrics helps you understand what's working and where you need to adjust. It's about being proactive and continuously improving your brand's effectiveness.

Leveraging personal branding for career growth is one of the most significant benefits. A strong brand makes you more attractive to employers, clients, and collaborators. It showcases your expertise and sets you apart from the competition. Whether you're looking for a job, a promotion, or new clients, a well-crafted personal brand is a powerful asset.

For entrepreneurs, personal branding is crucial. Your brand becomes synonymous with your business, influencing how people perceive your products or services. A strong personal brand can attract investors, customers, and media attention, giving your business a competitive edge. It's about building a brand that reflects your business values and vision.

Professionals across various fields can benefit from personal branding. Whether you're a lawyer, doctor, or engineer, your personal brand can enhance your reputation and open up new opportunities. It's about showcasing your expertise, building trust, and positioning yourself as a leader in your field.

Creatives, like artists, writers, and musicians, also need personal branding. In a competitive industry, a strong brand helps you stand out and attract fans, patrons, and collaborators. It's about creating a unique identity that resonates with your audience and reflects your artistic vision.

The future of personal branding is ever-evolving. With new technologies and platforms emerging, staying updated and adaptable is crucial. The basics of authenticity, consistency, and strategic communication remain the same, but the tools and methods will continue to change. Embracing these changes and continuously learning will keep your brand relevant and influential.

Your digital footprint is a crucial part of your personal brand. Everything you post online contributes to how people perceive you. Managing your digital footprint involves being mindful of what you share and how you interact online. It's about building a positive and professional presence that aligns with your brand values.

Protecting your personal brand is essential. This includes monitoring your online presence, addressing negative feedback professionally, and staying true to your values. Protecting your brand is about maintaining your reputation and ensuring that your message remains consistent and authentic.

Enhancing your personal brand through storytelling is powerful. Sharing your journey, challenges, and successes creates a connection with your audience. People relate to stories, and storytelling makes your brand memorable and engaging. It's about being real and sharing your unique experiences in a way that resonates with others.

Visuals play a significant role in personal branding. From your logo to the images you use on social media, visuals create a strong impression. Consistent and professional visuals enhance your brand's recognition and appeal. It's about creating a cohesive visual identity that reflects your brand's personality.

Collaborating with other brands can amplify your reach. Partnering with like-minded individuals or businesses can introduce you to new audiences and create exciting opportunities. It's about finding mutually beneficial collaborations that enhance your brand and bring value to your audience.

There are numerous tools and resources available to help you build and manage your personal brand. From social media management tools to online courses, leveraging these resources can make your branding efforts more effective and efficient. It's about using the right tools to support your strategy and streamline your efforts.

Getting started with personal branding can feel overwhelming, but remember, every big journey starts with a single step. Begin by defining your values, crafting your message, and setting your goals. Take small, consistent steps, and don't be afraid to learn and adjust as you go. Building a personal brand is a journey, not a destination, and it's one that can lead to incredible opportunities and growth.

As we dive deeper into the intricacies of personal branding, the next chapter will guide you through discovering your unique identity. This foundational step is crucial in building a brand that truly reflects who you are and resonates with your audience. So, let's embark on this journey of self-discovery and see how you can craft a powerful personal brand from the inside out.

Chapter 1: Discovering Your Unique Identity

Discovering your unique identity is like digging for buried treasure. It's all about uncovering what makes you special and different from everyone else. This journey begins with defining your core values. Your values are the principles that guide your decisions and actions. They are the foundation of your personal brand. Think about what matters most to you. Is it honesty, creativity, compassion, or something else? Identifying these values helps you stay true to yourself and build a brand that reflects your true self.

Knowing your strengths and weaknesses is also crucial. Everyone has areas where they excel and areas where they can improve. Understanding these helps you focus on what you do best and find ways to grow. It's like being a superhero who knows their powers and limitations. By acknowledging your weaknesses, you can work on them and turn them into strengths. This self-awareness is key to building a strong, authentic brand.

Finding your passion is another vital step. Passion is the fuel that drives you and keeps you motivated. It's what makes you excited to get up in the morning and work on your brand. Think about what you love to do, what you're good at, and what the world needs. Where these three intersect, you'll find your passion. Building a brand around your passion ensures that you'll stay committed and enthusiastic about your journey.

Creating a personal mission statement is like writing your own superhero motto. It's a clear, concise declaration of what you want to achieve and how you plan to do it. Your mission statement should reflect your values, strengths, and passions. It serves as a guiding light, helping you stay focused and aligned with your goals. A strong mission statement inspires you and those who follow your brand.

Analyzing your current online presence is a critical step in building your brand. Take a close look at what you've posted on social media, your website, and any other online platforms. Is your online presence consistent with the brand you want to build? If not, it's time to make some changes. Clean up any content that doesn't align with your brand values and start posting content that reflects your true self. Your online presence is often the first impression people have of you, so make it count.

Setting clear, achievable goals helps you stay on track and measure your progress. Your goals should be specific, measurable, achievable, relevant, and time-bound (SMART). For example, instead of saying, "I want to be famous," set a goal like, "I want to increase my LinkedIn followers by 10% in the next three months." Having clear goals gives you something to work towards and helps you stay focused on your branding journey.

Understanding your unique selling proposition (USP) is vital. Your USP is what sets you apart from others in your field. It's the unique value you offer that others don't. Think about what makes you different and how you can leverage that uniqueness to stand out. Whether it's your expertise, your personality, or your approach, your USP is a key part of your personal brand.

Conducting a personal SWOT analysis can provide valuable insights. SWOT stands for Strengths, Weaknesses, Opportunities, and Threats. By analyzing these areas, you can identify where you excel, where you can improve, opportunities you can seize, and challenges you need to overcome. This analysis helps you build a strategic plan for your personal brand.

The importance of self-awareness cannot be overstated. Being self-aware means understanding your emotions, motivations, and behaviors. It's about knowing how you affect others and how others perceive you. Self-awareness is the foundation of emotional intelligence, which is crucial for building strong relationships and a successful personal brand.

Leveraging feedback for self-improvement is essential. Ask for feedback from trusted friends, colleagues, and mentors. Listen to their insights and use them to improve your brand. Constructive feedback helps you grow and ensures that your brand remains relevant and effective. Don't be afraid of criticism; see it as an opportunity to learn and improve.

Aligning your personal and professional life ensures that your brand is authentic and sustainable. Your brand should reflect who you are in all aspects of your life. If there's a disconnect between your personal and professional identities, it can create confusion and mistrust. Strive for alignment to build a brand that is genuine and trustworthy.

Differentiating yourself from others is key to standing out. In a crowded market, being unique is crucial. Think about what makes you different and how you can highlight those differences in your brand. Whether it's your skills, your experiences, or your perspective, find what sets you apart and make it a central part of your brand.

Building confidence in your identity is a journey. Confidence comes from knowing who you are, what you stand for, and what you can offer. It's about embracing your strengths and working on your weaknesses. Confidence is attractive and helps you build a strong, compelling personal brand. Believe in yourself and others will too.

The role of personality in branding is significant. Your personality is what makes your brand relatable and memorable. It's about being yourself and letting your unique traits shine through. Whether you're funny, serious, quirky, or sophisticated, let your personality guide your brand. People connect with personalities, not just products or services.

Developing a growth mindset is crucial for personal branding. A growth mindset means believing that your abilities and intelligence can be developed through hard work and dedication. It's about embracing challenges, learning from failures, and continuously improving. A growth mindset helps you stay motivated and resilient on your branding journey.

Balancing authenticity and professionalism is important. While it's essential to be genuine, you also need to maintain a level of professionalism. This balance ensures that you're relatable and respected. It's about being real while also being mindful of how you present yourself in a professional context.

The impact of first impressions cannot be ignored. People form opinions about you within seconds of meeting you or seeing your online presence. Make sure your first impression aligns with your brand values and message. Whether it's your appearance, your online profiles, or your initial interactions, strive to make a positive and memorable first impression.

Crafting a compelling personal narrative is a powerful way to build your brand. Your narrative is the story of who you are, where you've been, and where you're going. It's about sharing your journey, your struggles, and your successes. A compelling narrative engages your audience and makes your brand more relatable and inspiring.

The significance of personal ethics in branding is paramount. Your ethics define your principles and guide your actions. Building a brand based on strong ethical values creates trust and respect. Be honest, transparent, and fair in all your dealings. Ethical branding not only enhances your reputation but also attracts like-minded followers and collaborators.

Embracing your individuality is key to creating a unique brand. Don't try to fit into someone else's mold. Celebrate what makes you different and let your individuality shine. Your unique perspective, experiences, and personality are your greatest assets. Embracing your individuality makes your brand stand out and resonate with your audience.

Overcoming imposter syndrome is a challenge many face. Imposter syndrome is the feeling that you're not good enough or that you don't deserve your success. It's important to recognize these feelings and work through them. Remember, everyone has moments of doubt. Focus on your achievements, seek support from mentors, and keep pushing forward.

Building resilience and adaptability is crucial for long-term success. Resilience helps you bounce back from setbacks, while adaptability allows you to adjust to changing circumstances. Together, these traits ensure that you can navigate challenges and continue growing your brand. Embrace change and see setbacks as opportunities to learn and improve.

Learning from role models and mentors can provide valuable guidance. Look up to individuals who have successfully built their personal brands. Study their strategies, learn from their experiences, and seek their advice. Mentors can offer insights, support, and encouragement, helping you navigate your branding journey more effectively.

The importance of lifelong learning cannot be overstated. The world is constantly changing, and staying relevant requires continuous learning. Seek out opportunities to expand your knowledge and skills. Whether it's through formal education, online courses, or reading, make learning a lifelong habit. Lifelong learning keeps your brand fresh and adaptable.

Aligning your brand with your goals ensures that your branding efforts are purposeful and effective. Your brand should reflect your aspirations and help you achieve your objectives. Regularly review your goals and adjust your branding strategy as needed. Alignment keeps your brand focused and driven towards success.

The power of self-reflection is immense. Taking time to reflect on your experiences, decisions, and progress helps you gain valuable insights. Self-reflection allows you to celebrate your successes, learn from your mistakes, and plan for the future. Make self-reflection a regular practice to keep your brand aligned and evolving.

Staying true to yourself in a digital world can be challenging but is essential. The digital world is full of noise and distractions, but staying authentic helps you stand out. Don't be swayed by trends or external pressures. Stick to your values, be genuine, and let your true self shine through. Authenticity builds trust and loyalty.

Personal branding in different cultures requires sensitivity and adaptability. Cultural differences can impact how your brand is perceived. Be mindful of cultural nuances and tailor your approach accordingly. Respecting and understanding different cultures enhances your brand's global appeal and fosters inclusivity.

Adapting your brand to various audiences ensures broader reach and impact. Different audiences have different needs and preferences. Tailor your message, tone, and approach to resonate with each audience segment. Adapting your brand makes it more relevant and engaging, helping you connect with a diverse range of people.

Celebrating your unique journey is important. Your branding journey is uniquely yours, filled with challenges, triumphs, and growth. Celebrate your milestones, big and small. Acknowledge your progress and take pride in your achievements. Celebrating your journey keeps you motivated and reminds you of how far you've come.

Now that we've explored the foundational aspects of discovering your unique identity, it's time to dive into the art of crafting your personal brand story. Your story is the heart of your brand, connecting you with your audience on a deeper level. Let's explore how to create a compelling narrative that resonates and inspires.

Chapter 2: Crafting Your Personal Brand Story

Crafting your personal brand story is like weaving a tapestry. It's about combining different threads of your experiences, values, and aspirations into a cohesive and compelling narrative. Your story is what sets you apart and makes your brand memorable. It's not just about listing your achievements; it's about sharing the journey, the challenges, and the triumphs that have shaped you.

The elements of a compelling story are simple yet powerful. Your story should have a clear beginning, middle, and end. The beginning introduces who you are and where you come from. The middle covers the challenges you've faced and the lessons you've learned. The end highlights where you are now and where you're headed. This structure makes your story engaging and relatable.

Finding your brand's voice is crucial. Your voice is the tone and style in which you communicate your story. It should reflect your personality and resonate with your audience. Whether your voice is formal, casual, humorous, or serious, consistency is key. Your voice sets the tone for your brand and helps build a connection with your audience.

Creating an emotional connection with your audience is essential. Emotions drive engagement and loyalty. Share the highs and lows of your journey, the moments of joy and the struggles. Be vulnerable and authentic. When people see the real you, they're more likely to connect with your brand on a deeper level. Emotional connection makes your story memorable and impactful.

Highlighting pivotal moments in your journey adds depth to your story. These are the turning points that have significantly impacted your life and career. Whether it's a major success, a failure, or a life-changing decision, these moments shape your narrative. Highlighting them shows your resilience and growth, making your story more relatable and inspiring.

Incorporating personal anecdotes makes your story more engaging. Anecdotes are short, personal stories that illustrate your experiences and values. They add a human touch to your narrative and make it more relatable. Share anecdotes that highlight your character, your values, and your journey. Personal stories make your brand more authentic and memorable.

The power of vulnerability in storytelling is immense. Being vulnerable means sharing your fears, mistakes, and challenges. It shows that you're human and that you've faced struggles just like everyone else. Vulnerability builds trust and connection. It's about being real and showing that success is not always a smooth journey. Embrace vulnerability to create a deeper bond with your audience.

Crafting a relatable narrative involves understanding your audience's needs and experiences. Your story should resonate with them and reflect their challenges and aspirations. Speak to their hearts and minds. Show that you understand their struggles and offer hope and inspiration. A relatable narrative makes your brand more engaging and impactful.

Balancing personal and professional stories is important. While it's essential to share your personal journey, your professional experiences also add value to your brand. Highlight your career achievements, your skills, and your expertise. Show how your personal and professional lives intersect and complement each other. This balance creates a well-rounded and compelling narrative.

Using storytelling for impact involves sharing stories that inspire and motivate your audience. Your story should not only be about you but also offer value to your audience. Share lessons learned, insights gained, and advice that can help others. Impactful storytelling makes your brand a source of inspiration and guidance.

The role of visuals in storytelling is significant. Visuals enhance your narrative and make it more engaging. Use photos, videos, and infographics to illustrate your story. Visuals bring your story to life and make it more memorable. They add a dynamic element to your narrative, making it more appealing and impactful.

Tailoring your story to different platforms ensures that it reaches a broader audience. Different platforms have different audiences and formats. Adapt your story to fit the platform, whether it's a blog, a social media post, or a video.

Tailoring your story makes it more relevant and engaging for each audience segment.

Keeping your story consistent across all platforms is crucial. Consistency builds trust and recognition. Ensure that your message, tone, and visuals are uniform across all platforms. A consistent story reinforces your brand identity and makes it more memorable. It helps your audience understand and connect with your brand more easily.

Evolving your story over time is necessary. As you grow and change, so should your story. Update your narrative to reflect new experiences, achievements, and lessons learned. Evolving your story keeps it relevant and engaging. It shows that you're continuously growing and adapting, which is inspiring for your audience.

The impact of storytelling on brand loyalty is profound. A compelling story creates an emotional connection with your audience, making them more loyal to your brand. When people resonate with your story, they're more likely to support and advocate for your brand. Storytelling builds a loyal and engaged community around your brand.

Using metaphors and analogies in your story makes it more vivid and relatable. Metaphors and analogies simplify complex ideas and create strong images in the minds of your audience. They make your story more engaging and memorable. Use them to illustrate your journey, your values, and your vision. They add depth and richness to your narrative.

The importance of a strong beginning in your story cannot be overstated. The beginning sets the stage and captures your audience's attention. Start with a powerful introduction that highlights who you are and what you stand for. A strong beginning draws your audience in and makes them want to hear more of your story.

Crafting a memorable ending is equally important. The ending should leave a lasting impression and inspire your audience. Highlight your current achievements and your vision for the future. A memorable ending reinforces your message and motivates your audience to take action. It leaves them with a sense of hope and inspiration.

Engaging your audience through storytelling involves creating a two-way conversation. Encourage your audience to share their stories, ask questions, and provide feedback. Engagement builds a sense of community and makes your brand more interactive. It shows that you value your audience's input and are open to learning from them.

Collecting and sharing testimonials adds credibility to your story. Testimonials from clients, colleagues, and mentors highlight your impact and achievements. They provide social proof and reinforce your brand's authenticity. Sharing testimonials shows that others believe in your brand and value your contributions.

The role of humor in storytelling is significant. Humor makes your story more relatable and enjoyable. It adds a light-hearted touch and makes your brand more approachable. Use humor to share your experiences, highlight your quirks, and connect with your audience. Humor builds a positive and engaging brand personality.

Using storytelling for problem-solving involves sharing stories that illustrate how you've overcome challenges. Highlight the problems you've faced and the solutions you've found. Problem-solving stories showcase your resilience, creativity, and expertise. They offer valuable insights and inspire your audience to overcome their challenges.

Building suspense and anticipation in your story keeps your audience engaged. Use cliffhangers, teasers, and plot twists to create excitement. Suspense and anticipation make your story more dynamic and compelling. They keep your audience hooked and eager to hear more. Use these elements to add drama and interest to your narrative.

The significance of authenticity in storytelling cannot be overstated. Authenticity builds trust and connection. Be true to yourself and share your real experiences. Don't try to create a perfect image; embrace your flaws and imperfections. Authentic storytelling makes your brand more relatable and trustworthy.

Overcoming challenges in storytelling involves being persistent and creative. Storytelling is not always easy, but it's worth the effort. Keep refining your narrative, seek feedback, and be open to new ideas. Overcoming challenges makes your story stronger and more impactful. It shows that you're committed to sharing your journey.

Learning from successful brand stories provides valuable insights. Study the stories of individuals and brands you admire. Analyze what makes their stories compelling and how they engage their audience. Learning from others helps you refine your own storytelling approach and build a more effective narrative.

Storytelling in public speaking is a powerful way to connect with your audience. Use your story to illustrate your points and engage your listeners. Public speaking offers a unique opportunity to share your narrative in a dynamic and interactive way. It enhances your brand's visibility and impact.

The power of multimedia storytelling is immense. Combining different media—text, images, videos, and audio—creates a rich and engaging narrative. Multimedia storytelling reaches a broader audience and enhances your story's impact. Use different media to share your experiences and connect with your audience on multiple levels.

Integrating your story into your content strategy ensures consistency and relevance. Your story should be the backbone of your content, guiding your posts, videos, and interactions. Integration creates a cohesive brand experience and reinforces your message. It makes your content more engaging and impactful.

Measuring the impact of your story involves looking at engagement metrics, feedback, and audience growth. Regularly review these metrics to understand what's working and where you can improve. Measuring impact helps you refine your storytelling approach and ensure that your narrative resonates with your audience.

Continuously refining your brand story is essential. Your story is a living, evolving narrative. Regularly update it to reflect new experiences and insights.

Refinement keeps your story fresh and relevant. It shows that you're continuously growing and adapting, which is inspiring for your audience.

Now that you've crafted a compelling personal brand story, it's time to build a strong online presence to share that story with the world. Your online presence is a powerful platform for promoting your brand, connecting with your audience, and showcasing your expertise. Let's explore how to build and maintain a dynamic and engaging online presence.

Chapter 3: Building Your Online Presence

Building your online presence is like constructing a digital home. It's where people come to learn about you, interact with your content, and engage with your brand. The foundation of a strong online presence is a professional website. Your website is your digital headquarters, where you can showcase your story, your work, and your expertise. Make sure it's well-designed, easy to navigate, and reflects your brand's personality.

Choosing the right social media platforms is crucial. Not all platforms are created equal, and each has its strengths. Identify where your audience spends their time and focus your efforts there. Whether it's LinkedIn for professional networking, Instagram for visual content, or Twitter for real-time updates, choose platforms that align with your brand and goals. Being strategic about your platform choices ensures that your efforts are effective and targeted.

Creating a professional website involves several key elements. Your website should have a clear and compelling homepage that introduces who you are and what you do. Include an about page that shares your story and your mission. A blog section allows you to share insights, updates, and valuable content with your audience. A portfolio or projects section showcases your work and achievements. Contact information and social media links make it easy for people to connect with you.

Optimizing your online profiles is essential. Your social media profiles should be complete, professional, and consistent with your brand. Use a high-quality profile picture and a compelling bio that highlights your expertise and values. Include links to your website and other relevant platforms. Regularly update your profiles with new content and engage with your audience. Optimized profiles enhance your credibility and make a strong first impression.

Developing a content strategy is key to maintaining a dynamic online presence. Your content strategy should outline what kind of content you'll create, how often you'll post, and which platforms you'll use. Focus on creating high-quality, valuable content that resonates with your audience. Whether it's blog posts, videos, infographics, or social media updates, your content should reflect your brand's message and values.

The importance of consistency in your online presence cannot be overstated. Consistency builds trust and recognition. Regularly update your website and social media profiles with fresh content. Maintain a consistent tone, style, and visual identity across all platforms. Consistency ensures that your audience knows what to expect and keeps your brand top of mind.

Engaging with your audience is a crucial part of building your online presence. Respond to comments, answer questions, and participate in conversations. Show appreciation for your followers and build a community around your brand. Engagement creates a two-way dialogue and makes your audience feel valued. It's about building relationships, not just broadcasting your message.

Building a personal blog is a powerful way to share your insights and expertise. A blog allows you to dive deeper into topics, share your thoughts, and provide valuable information to your audience. Regularly update your blog with new posts and promote them on your social media platforms. A well-maintained blog enhances your credibility and positions you as a thought leader in your field.

The role of SEO in personal branding is significant. SEO, or search engine optimization, helps your website and content rank higher in search engine results. This increases your visibility and attracts more visitors to your site. Use relevant keywords, create high-quality content, and optimize your website's structure and performance. SEO ensures that your brand is easily discoverable online.

Leveraging multimedia content makes your online presence more dynamic and engaging. Videos, podcasts, and infographics add variety and appeal to your content. They cater to different audience preferences and make your brand more versatile. Use multimedia to share your story, provide value, and connect with your audience in diverse ways.

The impact of visuals in your online presence is immense. High-quality images, graphics, and videos enhance your brand's appeal and make your content more engaging. Use visuals to illustrate your points, tell your story, and create a cohesive brand identity. Visuals make your content more memorable and shareable.

Using email marketing effectively can strengthen your online presence. Build an email list and regularly send out newsletters, updates, and valuable content. Email marketing allows you to maintain direct communication with your audience and build a loyal following. Personalize your emails and provide exclusive content to make your subscribers feel valued.

Networking online is a powerful way to expand your reach and build relationships. Join relevant online communities, participate in discussions, and connect with influencers in your field. Networking online allows you to share your expertise, learn from others, and create opportunities for collaboration. It's about being active and present in the digital spaces where your audience and peers gather.

Joining relevant online communities enhances your visibility and influence. Whether it's forums, social media groups, or professional networks, being part of a community allows you to engage with like-minded individuals, share your insights, and build your reputation. Active participation in online communities builds your brand and opens up new opportunities.

Participating in online discussions positions you as an engaged and knowledgeable individual. Share your thoughts, answer questions, and contribute valuable insights. Online discussions are a platform to showcase your expertise and connect with your audience. Being active in discussions enhances your credibility and makes your brand more relatable.

Collaborating with influencers can amplify your reach. Influencers have established audiences that trust their recommendations. Partnering with them allows you to tap into their audience and gain exposure. Choose influencers whose values and audience align with your brand. Collaborations can include guest posts, joint projects, or social media shoutouts.

Monitoring your online reputation is crucial. Regularly check what's being said about you and your brand online. Address negative feedback professionally and promptly. Celebrate and share positive feedback. Monitoring your reputation helps you maintain a positive image and address any issues before they escalate.

Responding to feedback and criticism professionally enhances your brand's credibility. Acknowledge feedback, thank the person for their input, and take appropriate action. Handling criticism with grace and professionalism shows that you value your audience's opinions and are committed to improving. It builds trust and respect for your brand.

Staying updated with digital trends ensures that your online presence remains relevant. The digital landscape is constantly evolving, and staying informed helps you adapt and leverage new opportunities. Follow industry blogs, attend webinars, and participate in online courses to stay current with the latest trends and best practices.

The power of online endorsements cannot be ignored. Endorsements from respected individuals or organizations add credibility to your brand. Encourage satisfied clients, colleagues, and mentors to endorse you on platforms like LinkedIn. Endorsements serve as social proof and enhance your reputation.

Creating valuable content is at the heart of a strong online presence. Your content should provide value to your audience, whether it's through information, inspiration, or entertainment. Focus on your audience's needs and interests. Valuable content attracts and retains followers, builds trust, and positions you as an authority in your field.

Using analytics to measure success is essential. Tools like Google Analytics and social media insights provide data on your audience's behavior, engagement, and preferences. Regularly review these metrics to understand what's working and where you can improve. Analytics helps you make informed decisions and refine your strategy.

The importance of a content calendar cannot be overstated. A content calendar helps you plan and organize your content, ensuring that you post regularly and consistently. It keeps you on track and allows you to align your content with your goals and audience's needs. A well-structured content calendar enhances your content strategy's effectiveness.

Maintaining professionalism online is crucial. Your online behavior reflects your brand, so always be respectful, courteous, and professional. Avoid controversial or offensive content. Professionalism builds trust and respect for your brand. It ensures that your online presence reflects positively on you and your brand.

Avoiding common online branding mistakes ensures that your efforts are effective. Common mistakes include inconsistent posting, ignoring feedback, and neglecting your website. Stay vigilant and proactive to avoid these pitfalls. Regularly review and refine your online presence to ensure it remains strong and effective.

Personal branding on LinkedIn involves optimizing your profile, sharing valuable content, and engaging with your network. LinkedIn is a powerful platform for professional branding, offering opportunities for networking, job searching, and showcasing your expertise. Regularly update your profile and participate in LinkedIn groups and discussions.

Personal branding on Instagram focuses on visual content. Use high-quality photos, videos, and graphics to tell your story and engage with your audience. Instagram Stories and Reels offer dynamic ways to share content and connect with your followers. Be consistent in your visual style and tone to create a cohesive brand identity.

Personal branding on Twitter involves sharing real-time updates, engaging in conversations, and using hashtags effectively. Twitter is great for quick, concise communication and staying current with industry trends. Participate in Twitter chats, follow relevant hashtags, and engage with influencers and peers.

Personal branding on Facebook involves creating a professional page, sharing valuable content, and engaging with your audience. Facebook Groups offer opportunities to connect with like-minded individuals and share your expertise. Use Facebook's analytics to understand your audience's preferences and refine your strategy.

Continuously improving your online presence is essential for long-term success. Regularly update your website, refresh your content, and stay active on social media. Seek feedback, learn from your analytics, and adapt to new trends.

Continuous improvement ensures that your online presence remains strong and relevant.

Now that we've explored how to build and maintain a strong online presence, let's dive into the art of content creation. Creating high-quality, engaging content is a powerful way to share your story, showcase your expertise, and connect with your audience. Let's dive into the strategies and techniques for effective content creation.

Chapter 4: Content Creation for Personal Branding

Content creation is like being an artist with a blank canvas. It's your opportunity to share your ideas, insights, and expertise with the world. High-quality content is the cornerstone of personal branding. It showcases your knowledge, builds trust, and engages your audience. The key to effective content creation is understanding your audience's needs and creating content that provides value.

Identifying your content niche is the first step. Your niche is the specific area or topic you'll focus on. It should align with your expertise, interests, and audience's needs. Narrowing down your niche helps you create targeted and relevant content. It positions you as an authority in your field and attracts a loyal following.

Creating a content plan ensures that your content is organized and consistent. Your plan should outline the topics you'll cover, the formats you'll use, and the schedule for publishing. A content plan keeps you on track and ensures that you regularly provide fresh content to your audience. It's about being strategic and intentional with your content efforts.

Writing compelling blog posts is a powerful way to share your insights and engage your audience. Your blog posts should be informative, well-researched, and written in a clear and engaging style. Use headlines, subheadings, and bullet points to break up the text and make it easy to read. Include images, videos, and links to enhance your posts and provide additional value.

Developing engaging social media content is essential for maintaining a strong online presence. Social media content should be visually appealing, concise, and shareable. Use a mix of text, images, videos, and graphics to keep your audience engaged. Regularly update your social media profiles with new content and interact with your followers to build a dynamic and active community.

The role of video content in personal branding is significant. Videos allow you to connect with your audience on a more personal level. They can be used to share insights, demonstrate skills, or provide behind-the-scenes glimpses into your life and work. Keep your videos short, engaging, and visually appealing. Use platforms like YouTube, Instagram, and Facebook to share your videos and reach a broader audience.

Podcasting for personal branding offers a unique way to share your expertise and connect with your audience. Podcasts allow you to dive deep into topics and provide valuable insights. They're also a great way to build relationships with other experts in your field through interviews and collaborations. Keep your podcasts informative, engaging, and relevant to your audience.

Creating shareable content increases your reach and visibility. Shareable content is engaging, valuable, and easy to share on social media. Infographics, memes, and listicles are examples of shareable content. Focus on creating content that resonates with your audience and encourages them to share it with their networks.

Using infographics and visuals enhances your content's appeal. Infographics present information in a visually engaging way, making it easier to understand and remember. Use infographics to share statistics, tips, and processes. High-quality visuals make your content more attractive and shareable, increasing your reach and impact.

The importance of storytelling in content cannot be overstated. Storytelling makes your content more engaging and relatable. Use stories to illustrate your points, share your experiences, and connect with your audience. Whether it's a blog post, a video, or a social media update, infuse your content with stories to make it more compelling.

Leveraging user-generated content adds authenticity to your brand. Encourage your audience to share their stories, experiences, and feedback. User-generated content not only provides social proof but also strengthens your community. Share and celebrate user-generated content to build a more inclusive and engaging brand.

Collaborating with content creators can amplify your reach and provide fresh perspectives. Partner with other bloggers, vloggers, and influencers to create joint content. Collaborations introduce you to new audiences and enhance your credibility. Choose collaborators who align with your brand values and audience interests.

Repurposing content across platforms maximizes its value. A single piece of content can be adapted into multiple formats. For example, a blog post can be turned into a video, an infographic, and social media updates. Repurposing content saves time and ensures that your message reaches a broader audience.

Keeping content relevant and timely ensures that it resonates with your audience. Stay updated with industry trends and current events to create content that's timely and relevant. Addressing trending topics and timely issues keeps your content fresh and engaging. It shows that you're in tune with what's happening in your field.

Balancing quantity and quality in content creation is crucial. While it's important to post regularly, never sacrifice quality for quantity. High-quality content provides value and builds trust. Focus on creating well-researched, informative, and engaging content. Quality content attracts and retains a loyal audience.

Using content to demonstrate expertise positions you as a thought leader in your field. Share insights, tips, and knowledge that showcase your expertise. Provide value to your audience by solving problems, answering questions, and offering guidance. Demonstrating expertise builds trust and credibility for your brand.

Engaging your audience with interactive content increases engagement and loyalty. Interactive content includes quizzes, polls, surveys, and live videos. It encourages your audience to participate and engage with your brand. Interactive content creates a dynamic and engaging brand experience.

The impact of live streaming on engagement is significant. Live streaming allows you to connect with your audience in real-time. Use live streams to share updates, host Q&A sessions, and provide behind-the-scenes glimpses. Live streaming builds a sense of immediacy and authenticity, enhancing your audience's connection with your brand.

Creating content series adds structure and anticipation to your content strategy. Content series are themed sets of posts, videos, or articles that cover a topic in depth over several installments. They create anticipation and encourage your audience to return for more. A well-planned content series enhances your content's impact and engagement.

Measuring content performance helps you understand what's working and where you can improve. Use analytics tools to track metrics like views, likes, shares, and comments. Regularly review these metrics to gain insights into your audience's preferences and behavior. Measuring performance helps you refine your content strategy and create more effective content.

The role of content curation in personal branding is significant. Content curation involves sharing valuable content from other sources that align with your brand. It positions you as a knowledgeable and resourceful individual. Curate content that provides value to your audience and complements your original content.

Using content to build relationships is a powerful strategy. Engage with your audience through comments, shares, and direct messages. Show appreciation for their feedback and contributions. Building relationships through content creates a loyal and engaged community around your brand.

Managing content creation tools helps streamline your efforts. Use tools for writing, graphic design, video editing, and social media management. Tools like Canva, Hootsuite, and Grammarly enhance your content creation process and improve efficiency. Managing the right tools ensures that your content is high-quality and professional.

Staying inspired and creative is essential for content creation. Regularly seek out new ideas, trends, and sources of inspiration. Attend conferences, read industry blogs, and connect with other content creators. Staying inspired keeps your content fresh and engaging. It ensures that you continue to provide value to your audience.

Handling content criticism gracefully is important. Not everyone will agree with or like your content. Be open to feedback and use it as an opportunity to improve. Address criticism professionally and constructively. Handling criticism gracefully enhances your credibility and shows that you value your audience's opinions.

Updating and refreshing old content ensures that it remains relevant and valuable. Regularly review your content library and update posts with new information, visuals, and insights. Refreshing old content gives it new life and increases its value. It shows that you're committed to providing accurate and up-to-date information.

Content for different stages of the buyer journey ensures that you meet your audience's needs at every stage. Create content that addresses awareness, consideration, and decision stages. Awareness content introduces your brand, consideration content provides in-depth information, and decision content encourages action. Tailoring content for each stage enhances its effectiveness.

Legal considerations in content creation are important. Ensure that your content complies with copyright laws, privacy regulations, and platform policies. Give proper credit for any third-party content you use. Understanding legal considerations protects your brand and maintains your credibility.

The future of content creation is ever-evolving. Stay informed about emerging trends, technologies, and best practices. Embrace new formats and platforms to keep your content fresh and relevant. The future of content creation offers endless opportunities for innovation and growth.

Building a sustainable content strategy ensures long-term success. Focus on creating high-quality content, engaging with your audience, and continuously improving. A sustainable strategy balances creativity, consistency, and efficiency. It ensures that your content efforts remain effective and impactful.

Now that we've covered the strategies and techniques for effective content creation, let's explore how to leverage social media for personal branding. Social media is a powerful tool for building your brand, connecting with your audience, and showcasing your content. Let's dive into the best practices and strategies for social media success.

Chapter 5: Social Media Strategies for Personal Branding

Social media is like a bustling marketplace where you can share your story, connect with your audience, and build your brand. It's a dynamic and powerful tool for personal branding. The first step in leveraging social media is choosing the right platforms. Different platforms serve different purposes, and it's important to focus your efforts where your audience is most active.

Developing a social media strategy ensures that your efforts are effective and aligned with your goals. Your strategy should outline your objectives, target audience, content themes, and posting schedule. A well-defined strategy keeps you on track and ensures that your social media efforts are purposeful and impactful.

Creating a consistent posting schedule is crucial for maintaining an active and engaging social media presence. Regularly posting content keeps your audience engaged and your brand top of mind. Use a content calendar to plan and schedule your posts. Consistency builds trust and ensures that your audience knows what to expect from you.

Engaging with your audience is key to building a loyal and active community. Respond to comments, answer questions, and participate in conversations. Show appreciation for your followers and acknowledge their contributions. Engagement creates a sense of community and makes your audience feel valued.

Using hashtags effectively increases your content's visibility and reach. Hashtags categorize your content and make it discoverable to a broader audience. Research and use relevant hashtags that align with your brand and content. Hashtags help you connect with new followers and expand your reach.

Leveraging social media analytics provides valuable insights into your audience's behavior and preferences. Use tools like Facebook Insights, Twitter Analytics, and Instagram Insights to track metrics like engagement, reach, and follower growth. Regularly review these metrics to understand what's working and where you can improve.

Running social media campaigns is a powerful way to promote your brand and achieve specific goals. Campaigns can include contests, giveaways, challenges, and collaborations. Define clear objectives for your campaigns and measure their success. Social media campaigns create excitement and engagement around your brand.

Collaborating with influencers can amplify your reach and credibility. Influencers have established audiences that trust their recommendations. Partnering with them allows you to tap into their audience and gain exposure. Choose influencers whose values and audience align with your brand. Collaborations can include guest posts, joint projects, or social media shoutouts.

Building a community on social media involves creating a space where your audience can connect, share, and engage. Use features like Facebook Groups, LinkedIn Groups, and Instagram Communities to foster interaction. Building a community creates a loyal and engaged following that supports and promotes your brand.

Using social media for networking is a powerful strategy. Connect with industry leaders, peers, and potential collaborators. Participate in discussions, share your insights, and build relationships. Networking on social media opens up new opportunities and enhances your brand's visibility.

Creating shareable content increases your reach and engagement. Shareable content is engaging, valuable, and easy to share on social media. Infographics, memes, and listicles are examples of shareable content. Focus on creating content that resonates with your audience and encourages them to share it with their networks.

The role of visuals in social media is significant. High-quality images, graphics, and videos enhance your content's appeal and engagement. Use visuals to illustrate your points, tell your story, and create a cohesive brand identity. Visuals make your content more memorable and shareable.

Handling negative feedback professionally is crucial for maintaining a positive online reputation. Acknowledge the feedback, thank the person for their input, and address the issue constructively. Handling negative feedback with grace and professionalism shows that you value your audience's opinions and are committed to improving.

Staying authentic on social media builds trust and connection. Be genuine in your interactions and share your real experiences. Don't try to create a perfect image; embrace your flaws and imperfections. Authenticity makes your brand more relatable and trustworthy.

Personal branding on LinkedIn involves optimizing your profile, sharing valuable content, and engaging with your network. LinkedIn is a powerful platform for professional branding, offering opportunities for networking, job searching, and showcasing your expertise. Regularly update your profile and participate in LinkedIn groups and discussions.

Personal branding on Instagram focuses on visual content. Use high-quality photos, videos, and graphics to tell your story and engage with your audience. Instagram Stories and Reels offer dynamic ways to share content and connect with your followers. Be consistent in your visual style and tone to create a cohesive brand identity.

Personal branding on Twitter involves sharing real-time updates, engaging in conversations, and using hashtags effectively. Twitter is great for quick, concise communication and staying current with industry trends. Participate in Twitter chats, follow relevant hashtags, and engage with influencers and peers.

Personal branding on Facebook involves creating a professional page, sharing valuable content, and engaging with your audience. Facebook Groups offer opportunities to connect with like-minded individuals and share your expertise. Use Facebook's analytics to understand your audience's preferences and refine your strategy.

Using stories and reels on platforms like Instagram and Facebook adds a dynamic and engaging element to your content strategy. Stories and reels are short, engaging videos that capture your audience's attention. Use them to share updates, behind-the-scenes glimpses, and interactive content. Stories and reels increase your content's reach and engagement.

Live streaming for engagement is a powerful way to connect with your audience in real-time. Use live streams to share updates, host Q&A sessions, and provide behind-the-scenes glimpses. Live streaming builds a sense of immediacy and authenticity, enhancing your audience's connection with your brand.

Managing multiple social media accounts can be challenging but is necessary for reaching different audience segments. Use social media management tools to streamline your efforts and ensure consistency. Managing multiple accounts effectively enhances your brand's visibility and engagement.

The importance of social media etiquette cannot be overstated. Always be respectful, courteous, and professional in your interactions. Avoid controversial or offensive content. Social media etiquette builds trust and respect for your brand. It ensures that your online presence reflects positively on you and your brand.

Avoiding social media burnout is crucial for maintaining a sustainable presence. Social media can be demanding and time-consuming. Set boundaries, take breaks, and prioritize self-care. Avoiding burnout ensures that you can maintain an active and engaging social media presence in the long term.

The role of social media ads in personal branding is significant. Social media ads allow you to reach a broader audience and promote your content. Use targeted ads to reach specific demographics and achieve your branding goals. Social media ads enhance your visibility and attract new followers.

Building relationships with followers involves engaging with them regularly, showing appreciation, and providing value. Respond to comments, acknowledge their contributions, and create opportunities for interaction. Building relationships creates a loyal and engaged following that supports and promotes your brand.

Measuring social media ROI (return on investment) helps you understand the effectiveness of your efforts. Track metrics like engagement, reach, follower growth, and conversions. Regularly review these metrics to understand what's working and where you can improve. Measuring ROI ensures that your social media strategy remains effective.

Staying updated with social media changes ensures that your strategy remains relevant. Social media platforms regularly update their features and algorithms. Stay informed about these changes and adapt your strategy accordingly. Staying updated ensures that you can leverage new opportunities and maintain an effective presence.

Legal considerations for social media involve understanding platform policies, copyright laws, and privacy regulations. Ensure that your content complies with these rules. Understanding legal considerations protects your brand and maintains your credibility.

The future of social media for personal branding offers endless opportunities. Embrace new platforms, formats, and trends to keep your strategy fresh and effective. The future of social media is dynamic and evolving, offering exciting opportunities for innovation and growth.

Now that we've explored the best practices and strategies for leveraging social media, let's dive into the art of networking and relationship building. Building strong relationships is essential for personal branding, and networking offers valuable opportunities to connect, collaborate, and grow. Let's explore how to effectively network and build meaningful relationships.

Chapter 6: Networking and Relationship Building

Networking and relationship building are like planting seeds. They take time and effort to grow, but they yield valuable connections and opportunities. The importance of networking in personal branding cannot be overstated. Networking allows you to connect with like-minded individuals, share your expertise, and create opportunities for collaboration. It's about building a community that supports and promotes your brand.

Building your network online and offline involves attending events, joining groups, and engaging in conversations. Online networking can include social media interactions, virtual conferences, and webinars. Offline networking involves attending industry events, workshops, and meetups. Both online and offline networking are essential for building a diverse and robust network.

Developing strong relationships requires genuine interest and effort. Take the time to get to know people, understand their needs, and offer your support. Strong relationships are built on trust, mutual respect, and shared values. They require ongoing effort and communication to maintain.

Leveraging your existing network can open up new opportunities. Reach out to your contacts for introductions, advice, and collaborations. Your existing network is a valuable resource for expanding your reach and building new relationships. Nurture these connections and show appreciation for their support.

Networking at events and conferences provides valuable opportunities to connect with industry leaders and peers. Attend relevant events, participate in discussions, and share your insights. Events and conferences offer a platform to showcase your expertise, learn from others, and build meaningful connections.

Using LinkedIn for networking is a powerful strategy. LinkedIn is a professional networking platform that allows you to connect with industry leaders, peers, and potential collaborators. Optimize your profile, join groups, and participate in discussions. Regularly update your profile and engage with your network to build a strong LinkedIn presence.

The power of networking groups cannot be ignored. Join relevant networking groups on platforms like LinkedIn, Facebook, and Meetup. These groups offer opportunities to connect with like-minded individuals, share your expertise, and collaborate on projects. Networking groups provide a supportive community that enhances your personal brand.

Giving before you receive is a key principle in networking. Offer your support, share your expertise, and provide value to your connections. Giving creates a positive impression and builds goodwill. It shows that you're genuinely interested in building meaningful relationships, not just looking for personal gain.

Following up effectively is crucial for maintaining and strengthening your connections. After meeting someone new, send a follow-up message to express your appreciation and continue the conversation. Regularly check in with your connections and stay updated on their achievements. Following up shows that you value the relationship and are committed to staying connected.

Building a personal CRM (customer relationship management) system helps you manage your network. Use a CRM tool to keep track of your connections, interactions, and follow-ups. A personal CRM system ensures that you stay organized and maintain strong relationships with your network.

Networking for introverts can be challenging but is essential for personal branding. Introverts can leverage their strengths, such as listening and building deep connections, to network effectively. Focus on one-on-one interactions, online networking, and attending smaller events. Networking for introverts involves finding strategies that align with their strengths and comfort levels.

The role of mentors in networking is significant. Mentors provide guidance, support, and valuable insights. Seek out mentors who have successfully built their personal brands and learn from their experiences. Mentors can offer advice, introduce you to new opportunities, and help you navigate challenges.

Networking with influencers enhances your brand's visibility and credibility. Influencers have established audiences that trust their recommendations. Building relationships with influencers allows you to tap into their network and gain exposure. Engage with influencers by sharing their content, participating in discussions, and offering your support.

Maintaining professional relationships requires ongoing effort and communication. Regularly check in with your connections, show appreciation for their support, and offer your assistance. Strong professional relationships are built on trust, mutual respect, and consistent communication. They require effort to maintain but yield valuable opportunities and support.

Networking through volunteering offers unique opportunities to connect with like-minded individuals. Volunteer for causes and organizations that align with your values and interests. Volunteering allows you to give back to the community while building meaningful relationships. It shows that you're committed to making a positive impact and enhances your personal brand.

The impact of networking on personal branding is profound. Networking enhances your visibility, credibility, and influence. It opens up new opportunities for collaboration, learning, and growth. Building a strong network supports your personal branding efforts and creates a supportive community around your brand.

Building relationships through content involves engaging with your audience and creating opportunities for interaction. Share valuable content, respond to comments, and participate in discussions. Building relationships through content creates a loyal and engaged following that supports and promotes your brand.

Using email for relationship building is a powerful strategy. Regularly send out newsletters, updates, and personalized messages to your network. Email allows you to maintain direct communication and build stronger relationships. Personalize your emails and provide exclusive content to make your subscribers feel valued.

Hosting networking events provides opportunities to connect with your audience and build your brand. Host webinars, virtual meetups, or in-person events to share your expertise and engage with your network. Hosting events positions you as a leader in your field and enhances your visibility and influence.

The importance of a personal pitch cannot be overstated. Your personal pitch is a concise and compelling summary of who you are, what you do, and what you offer. It should highlight your unique value and create a positive impression. Practice your pitch and use it in networking interactions to introduce yourself effectively.

Being authentic in networking builds trust and connection. Be genuine in your interactions and share your real experiences. Don't try to create a perfect image; embrace your flaws and imperfections. Authenticity makes your brand more relatable and trustworthy, enhancing your networking efforts.

Leveraging social media for networking is a powerful strategy. Use platforms like LinkedIn, Twitter, and Instagram to connect with industry leaders, peers, and potential collaborators. Engage in discussions, share your insights, and build relationships. Social media offers endless opportunities for networking and relationship building.

Networking with industry leaders enhances your visibility and credibility. Connect with leaders in your field, share your insights, and learn from their experiences. Building relationships with industry leaders opens up new opportunities and enhances your personal brand.

Building a diverse network ensures that you have a broad range of connections and opportunities. Connect with individuals from different backgrounds, industries, and perspectives. A diverse network enhances your learning, expands your reach, and creates a richer and more inclusive brand.

The role of networking in career growth is significant. Networking opens up new opportunities for job searching, promotions, and collaborations. It provides valuable insights, support, and guidance. Building a strong network supports your career growth and enhances your personal branding efforts.

Overcoming networking challenges involves being persistent and creative. Networking can be intimidating, but it's essential for personal branding. Find strategies that align with your strengths and comfort levels. Overcoming challenges in networking shows your commitment to building meaningful relationships.

The power of small talk in networking should not be underestimated. Small talk builds rapport and opens up conversations. Use small talk to connect with new people, find common interests, and create a positive impression. Small talk is a valuable tool for building relationships.

Building long-term relationships requires ongoing effort and communication. Regularly check in with your connections, show appreciation for their support, and offer your assistance. Long-term relationships are built on trust, mutual respect, and consistent communication. They require effort to maintain but yield valuable opportunities and support.

The importance of listening in networking cannot be overstated. Listening shows that you value the other person's perspective and are genuinely interested in what they have to say. Active listening builds trust and strengthens relationships. It enhances your networking efforts and creates a positive impression.

Celebrating your network involves acknowledging and appreciating the support and contributions of your connections. Celebrate their achievements, show gratitude for their support, and create opportunities for collaboration. Celebrating your network builds goodwill and strengthens your relationships.

Now that we've explored the strategies for effective networking and relationship building, let's dive into the art of managing your online reputation. Your online reputation is a critical aspect of your personal brand, and managing it effectively ensures that you maintain a positive and professional image. Let's explore the best practices and strategies for online reputation management.

Chapter 7: Managing Your Online Reputation

Managing your online reputation is like tending to a garden. It requires regular attention and care to ensure that it flourishes. Your online reputation is a critical aspect of your personal brand, and managing it effectively ensures that you maintain a positive and professional image. Understanding online reputation management is the first step. It involves monitoring your online presence, addressing feedback, and proactively building a positive image.

The impact of your digital footprint cannot be overstated. Everything you post online contributes to how people perceive you. Your digital footprint includes social media posts, blog articles, comments, and any other online interactions. Managing your digital footprint involves being mindful of what you share and how you interact online. It's about building a positive and professional presence that aligns with your brand values.

Monitoring your online presence is crucial for maintaining a positive reputation. Regularly check what's being said about you and your brand online. Use tools like Google Alerts and social media monitoring tools to track mentions and reviews. Monitoring your presence helps you stay informed and address any issues promptly.

Responding to feedback and criticism professionally is essential for maintaining your reputation. Acknowledge feedback, thank the person for their input, and address the issue constructively. Handling criticism with grace and professionalism shows that you value your audience's opinions and are committed to improving. It builds trust and respect for your brand.

Building a positive online image involves proactively sharing content that reflects your values and expertise. Share your achievements, insights, and experiences. Engage with your audience and provide value through your content. A positive online image enhances your credibility and attracts followers and supporters.

Handling negative reviews requires a strategic approach. Acknowledge the review, apologize if necessary, and offer a solution. Avoid getting defensive or argumentative. Addressing negative reviews professionally shows that you're committed to providing excellent service and improving based on feedback.

The role of transparency in reputation management is significant. Being transparent builds trust and credibility. Share your processes, values, and challenges openly. Transparency shows that you're genuine and trustworthy. It enhances your reputation and creates a loyal and engaged following.

Protecting your personal information online is crucial for maintaining your reputation. Be mindful of what personal information you share and who you share it with. Use privacy settings on social media and other platforms to control who can see your information. Protecting your personal information ensures that your online presence remains secure and professional.

Using SEO for reputation management increases your visibility and ensures that positive content about you ranks higher in search engine results. Create high-quality content, use relevant keywords, and optimize your website's structure and performance. SEO helps you control your online narrative and maintain a positive image.

Leveraging positive content enhances your online reputation. Share your achievements, testimonials, and endorsements. Positive content serves as social proof and reinforces your credibility. It creates a positive impression and attracts followers and supporters.

Engaging with your audience is a crucial part of reputation management. Respond to comments, answer questions, and participate in conversations. Show appreciation for your followers and build a community around your brand. Engagement creates a positive and interactive brand experience.

Addressing misinformation promptly and professionally is essential for maintaining your reputation. If you come across false or misleading information about you or your brand, address it calmly and provide the correct information. Correcting misinformation shows that you're proactive and committed to maintaining your reputation.

Building trust online involves consistently delivering on your promises and providing value to your audience. Trust is built through honesty, transparency, and reliability. Regularly engage with your audience, share valuable content, and be responsive to feedback. Building trust enhances your reputation and creates a loyal following.

Managing your brand's voice ensures that your communication is consistent and professional. Your brand's voice should reflect your values and personality. Whether it's formal, casual, humorous, or serious, maintain consistency across all platforms. A consistent brand voice builds trust and recognition.

The importance of consistency in reputation management cannot be overstated. Consistency in your message, tone, and visuals builds trust and recognition. Regularly update your online profiles, share fresh content, and engage with your audience. Consistency ensures that your audience knows what to expect and trusts your brand.

Using social media for reputation management involves monitoring mentions, addressing feedback, and sharing positive content. Social media is a powerful tool for building and maintaining your online reputation. Be active on your platforms, engage with your audience, and use social media analytics to measure your efforts.

The role of public relations in reputation management is significant. Public relations involves managing your brand's image and relationships with the public. Use PR strategies to share your achievements, handle crises, and build positive relationships with the media. Effective PR enhances your reputation and creates positive publicity.

Crisis management strategies are essential for handling unexpected challenges. Have a plan in place for addressing crises, whether it's negative publicity, social media backlash, or other issues. Respond promptly, communicate transparently, and take responsibility if necessary. Effective crisis management minimizes damage and protects your reputation.

Learning from reputation management case studies provides valuable insights. Study how other individuals and brands have handled reputation challenges.

Analyze what worked and what didn't. Learning from others helps you develop effective strategies and avoid common pitfalls.

Legal considerations in reputation management involve understanding defamation, privacy laws, and platform policies. Ensure that your content complies with legal regulations. Understanding legal considerations protects your brand and maintains your credibility.

The impact of online reputation on opportunities cannot be ignored. A positive online reputation attracts job offers, collaborations, and other opportunities. It enhances your credibility and makes you a more attractive candidate. Managing your reputation effectively ensures that you capitalize on these opportunities.

Building a positive narrative involves sharing your story, achievements, and values. Your narrative should reflect who you are and what you stand for. Share your journey, your challenges, and your successes. A positive narrative enhances your reputation and makes your brand more relatable and inspiring.

The role of testimonials in reputation management is significant. Testimonials provide social proof and reinforce your credibility. Encourage satisfied clients, colleagues, and mentors to share their experiences. Share testimonials on your website, social media, and other platforms to enhance your reputation.

Managing your personal brand during transitions involves being transparent and proactive. Whether it's a career change, a new project, or a rebranding effort, communicate openly with your audience. Share your reasons for the change and how it aligns with your values and goals. Managing transitions effectively ensures that your reputation remains strong.

The power of a professional online presence cannot be overstated. A professional online presence enhances your credibility and attracts opportunities. Regularly update your profiles, share high-quality content, and engage with your audience. A professional online presence reflects positively on you and your brand.

Building a reputation management plan ensures that you're proactive and prepared. Your plan should include monitoring your online presence, addressing feedback, and sharing positive content. Regularly review and update your plan to ensure that it remains effective. A reputation management plan protects and enhances your brand.

The future of online reputation management offers exciting opportunities. With new tools, platforms, and strategies emerging, staying updated is crucial. Embrace new technologies and best practices to enhance your reputation management efforts. The future of reputation management is dynamic and evolving, offering endless opportunities for growth.

Leveraging technology for reputation management enhances your efforts. Use tools for monitoring, analytics, and content creation. Technology streamlines your efforts and ensures that you're proactive and effective. Leveraging technology enhances your reputation management strategy.

The importance of continuous improvement in reputation management cannot be overstated. Regularly review your efforts, seek feedback, and make adjustments as needed. Continuous improvement ensures that your reputation management strategy remains effective and impactful.

Celebrating your reputation management successes is important. Acknowledge and celebrate the positive feedback, achievements, and milestones. Celebrating successes builds motivation and reinforces your commitment to maintaining a positive reputation.

Now that we've explored the best practices and strategies for managing your online reputation, let's dive into leveraging technology and tools for personal branding. Technology offers endless opportunities to enhance your branding efforts, streamline your processes, and reach a broader audience. Let's explore how to leverage technology and tools effectively.

Chapter 8: Leveraging Technology and Tools

Leveraging technology and tools for personal branding is like having a superpower. Technology enhances your efforts, streamlines your processes, and expands your reach. The role of technology in personal branding is significant, offering endless opportunities for innovation and growth. Understanding the essential tools for personal branding is the first step. These tools help you manage your online presence, create content, and engage with your audience effectively.

Using social media management tools streamlines your efforts. Tools like Hootsuite, Buffer, and Sprout Social allow you to schedule posts, monitor mentions, and analyze your performance. Social media management tools ensure that you maintain a consistent and active presence across platforms. They save time and enhance your social media strategy.

Leveraging analytics and insights provides valuable data on your audience's behavior and preferences. Tools like Google Analytics, Facebook Insights, and Twitter Analytics track metrics like engagement, reach, and conversions. Regularly review these insights to understand what's working and where you can improve. Analytics helps you make informed decisions and refine your strategy.

Tools for content creation enhance your ability to produce high-quality content. Tools like Canva for graphic design, Grammarly for writing, and Adobe Premiere for video editing make content creation more accessible and professional. Using the right tools ensures that your content is visually appealing, well-written, and engaging.

Email marketing platforms like Mailchimp, Constant Contact, and ConvertKit help you build and manage your email list. Email marketing allows you to maintain direct communication with your audience and build a loyal following. Use email marketing platforms to create newsletters, automated campaigns, and personalized messages. Email marketing enhances your engagement and builds stronger relationships with your audience.

Building a professional website is a cornerstone of personal branding. Website builders like WordPress, Wix, and Squarespace make it easy to create a professional and visually appealing site. Your website should showcase your story, your work, and your expertise. Regularly update your website with new content and ensure that it reflects your brand's personality.

SEO tools and techniques enhance your website's visibility and attract more visitors. Tools like Ahrefs, SEMrush, and Yoast SEO help you optimize your content for search engines. Use relevant keywords, create high-quality content, and improve your site's structure and performance. SEO ensures that your brand is easily discoverable online.

Using CRM systems for relationship management helps you keep track of your connections and interactions. CRM tools like Salesforce, HubSpot, and Zoho CRM allow you to manage your network, follow up effectively, and build stronger relationships. A CRM system ensures that you stay organized and maintain strong connections with your network.

Project management tools streamline your efforts and enhance your productivity. Tools like Trello, Asana, and Monday.com help you manage tasks, collaborate with others, and stay on track with your goals. Project management tools ensure that your projects are well-organized and efficiently executed.

Multimedia creation tools like Adobe Creative Cloud, Final Cut Pro, and Audacity enhance your ability to create high-quality videos, graphics, and audio content. Multimedia content adds variety and appeal to your brand. Use these tools to create engaging and professional content that resonates with your audience.

Leveraging AI and automation enhances your branding efforts. AI tools like chatbots, predictive analytics, and content recommendation engines provide personalized experiences for your audience. Automation tools like Zapier and IFTTT streamline repetitive tasks and improve efficiency. AI and automation enhance your ability to engage with your audience and deliver value.

The impact of mobile apps on personal branding is significant. Mobile apps like Instagram, TikTok, and Clubhouse offer dynamic and engaging platforms for sharing your content and connecting with your audience. Use mobile apps to stay active and present in the digital spaces where your audience spends their time.

Online courses and learning platforms provide opportunities for continuous learning and growth. Platforms like Coursera, Udemy, and LinkedIn Learning offer courses on various topics, from digital marketing to personal development. Regularly invest in your learning to stay updated and enhance your skills. Continuous learning keeps your brand fresh and relevant.

Using webinars and online events to engage with your audience provides dynamic opportunities for interaction. Host webinars, virtual meetups, and online workshops to share your expertise, answer questions, and connect with your audience. Webinars and online events build a sense of community and enhance your brand's visibility and influence.

Podcasting tools and platforms like Anchor, Podbean, and Libsyn make it easy to create and share podcasts. Podcasting offers a unique way to share your insights, connect with your audience, and build relationships with other experts in your field. Use podcasting tools to create high-quality and engaging episodes that resonate with your audience.

E-commerce tools for personal branding allow you to monetize your brand effectively. Platforms like Shopify, WooCommerce, and Etsy enable you to sell products and services online. Use e-commerce tools to create an online store, manage inventory, and process payments. E-commerce enhances your ability to generate revenue and grow your brand.

Tools for online security are crucial for protecting your personal information and maintaining a professional online presence. Use tools like LastPass, Norton Security, and VPNs to safeguard your data. Online security ensures that your online presence remains secure and professional.

Collaboration tools and platforms like Slack, Microsoft Teams, and Zoom facilitate communication and collaboration with your team and network. Use these tools to share ideas, manage projects, and stay connected. Collaboration tools enhance your productivity and ensure that your projects run smoothly.

The role of cloud storage in personal branding is significant. Tools like Google Drive, Dropbox, and OneDrive provide secure and accessible storage for your files and documents. Cloud storage ensures that your content is safe, organized, and accessible from anywhere. It enhances your ability to manage your digital assets effectively.

Virtual meeting tools like Zoom, Google Meet, and Microsoft Teams provide opportunities for real-time communication and collaboration. Use virtual meeting tools to host webinars, conduct meetings, and engage with your audience. Virtual meetings enhance your ability to connect and collaborate effectively.

Managing your digital assets involves organizing and maintaining your content, files, and data. Use tools like DAM (Digital Asset Management) systems to manage your digital assets efficiently. Organized digital assets ensure that your content is easily accessible and well-maintained.

Tools for online reputation management like Brand24, Mention, and Reputology help you monitor your online presence and address feedback. Use these tools to track mentions, analyze sentiment, and manage your reputation effectively. Online reputation management tools ensure that you maintain a positive and professional image.

Leveraging technology for networking enhances your ability to connect with like-minded individuals and build relationships. Use platforms like LinkedIn, Twitter, and Clubhouse to engage with industry leaders, peers, and potential collaborators. Technology offers endless opportunities for networking and relationship building.

The future of personal branding tools offers exciting opportunities for innovation and growth. With new technologies and platforms emerging, staying updated is crucial. Embrace new tools and best practices to enhance your branding efforts. The future of personal branding is dynamic and evolving, offering endless opportunities for growth and success.

Integrating tools into your strategy ensures that your efforts are streamlined and effective. Choose the right tools for your needs and integrate them into your workflow. Regularly review and update your toolset to ensure that it remains relevant and effective. Integration enhances your productivity and ensures that your branding efforts are impactful.

Choosing the right tools for your needs involves understanding your goals, preferences, and budget. Evaluate different tools based on their features, ease of use, and cost. Choosing the right tools ensures that you have the resources you need to succeed. It enhances your ability to create, manage, and promote your brand effectively.

Staying updated with technology trends ensures that your branding efforts remain relevant and effective. Follow industry blogs, attend webinars, and participate in online courses to stay informed about the latest trends and best practices. Staying updated keeps your strategy fresh and innovative.

The impact of technology on personal branding is profound. Technology enhances your ability to create, share, and promote your content. It expands your reach and provides new opportunities for engagement and growth. Leveraging technology effectively ensures that your branding efforts are successful and impactful.

Now that we've explored the strategies for leveraging technology and tools for personal branding, let's dive into the art of monetizing your personal brand. Monetizing your brand offers opportunities to generate revenue, expand your reach, and enhance your impact. Let's explore the best practices and strategies for effective brand monetization.

Chapter 9: Monetizing Your Personal Brand

Monetizing your personal brand is like turning your passion into profit. It's about leveraging your expertise, content, and influence to generate revenue. Understanding brand monetization is the first step. Brand monetization involves creating products, offering services, and leveraging partnerships to generate income. It's about finding the right opportunities that align with your brand values and audience needs.

Identifying monetization opportunities involves understanding your audience's needs and preferences. What products or services would they find valuable? How can you leverage your expertise to provide value? Identifying the right opportunities ensures that your monetization efforts are effective and aligned with your brand.

Creating digital products is a powerful way to monetize your brand. Digital products can include eBooks, online courses, webinars, and templates. They provide valuable content that your audience can access and benefit from. Creating digital products allows you to share your expertise and generate passive income.

Offering consulting services leverages your expertise to provide personalized guidance and support. Consulting services can include one-on-one coaching, group sessions, and workshops. Offering consulting services allows you to build relationships with your clients and provide tailored solutions to their needs.

Monetizing through content creation involves generating revenue from your content. This can include sponsored posts, affiliate marketing, and ad revenue. Platforms like YouTube, Instagram, and blogs offer opportunities to monetize your content. Focus on creating high-quality, engaging content that attracts sponsors and partners.

Building online courses allows you to share your knowledge and expertise with a broader audience. Online courses provide valuable learning experiences and generate passive income. Use platforms like Teachable, Udemy, and Thinkific to create and sell your courses. Building online courses positions you as an authority in your field and enhances your brand's impact.

Publishing books and eBooks is a powerful way to share your story and expertise. Books and eBooks provide valuable content that your audience can access and benefit from. Use platforms like Amazon Kindle Direct Publishing, Barnes & Noble Press, and IngramSpark to publish and sell your books. Publishing books enhances your credibility and generates revenue.

Speaking engagements and workshops offer opportunities to share your expertise and connect with your audience. Speaking engagements can include conferences, webinars, and corporate events. Workshops provide interactive learning experiences. Speaking engagements and workshops enhance your visibility and generate income.

Affiliate marketing strategies involve promoting products or services and earning a commission on sales. Choose affiliate products that align with your brand and audience's needs. Use platforms like Amazon Associates, ShareASale, and CJ Affiliate to find affiliate opportunities. Affiliate marketing provides a passive income stream and adds value to your audience.

Sponsored content and partnerships involve collaborating with brands to create content that promotes their products or services. Sponsored content can include blog posts, social media updates, and videos. Choose partners that align with your brand values and audience's interests. Sponsored content and partnerships generate revenue and enhance your credibility.

Creating a membership site provides exclusive content and benefits to your audience. Membership sites can include access to premium content, community forums, and special events. Use platforms like Patreon, MemberPress, and Substack to create and manage your membership site. Membership sites generate recurring revenue and build a loyal community.

Leveraging your expertise involves creating products and services that showcase your knowledge and skills. This can include coaching programs, workshops, and digital products. Leveraging your expertise enhances your credibility and provides valuable solutions to your audience.

Selling merchandise allows you to create branded products that your audience can purchase. Merchandise can include apparel, accessories, and digital products. Use platforms like Shopify, Etsy, and Printful to create and sell your merchandise. Selling merchandise generates revenue and enhances your brand's visibility.

Building a subscription service provides regular content and benefits to your audience. Subscription services can include access to exclusive content, newsletters, and community forums. Use platforms like Substack, Patreon, and Kajabi to create and manage your subscription service. Subscription services generate recurring revenue and build a loyal following.

Crowdfunding and donations offer opportunities to generate revenue and support your projects. Use platforms like Kickstarter, GoFundMe, and Patreon to launch crowdfunding campaigns. Encourage your audience to support your projects through donations. Crowdfunding and donations provide financial support and enhance your community's engagement.

The role of advertisements in brand monetization is significant. Use platforms like Google AdSense, Facebook Ads, and YouTube Ads to generate ad revenue. Advertisements provide a passive income stream and enhance your content's visibility. Ensure that your ads align with your brand values and audience's interests.

Licensing your brand involves allowing other companies to use your brand's name, logo, or content for a fee. Licensing can include merchandise, digital products, and content. Licensing generates revenue and enhances your brand's visibility. Ensure that your licensing agreements align with your brand values and goals.

Monetizing through social media involves leveraging your social media presence to generate revenue. This can include sponsored posts, affiliate marketing, and social media ads. Use platforms like Instagram, Facebook, and YouTube to monetize your social media content. Social media monetization enhances your reach and provides a passive income stream.

The impact of monetization on your brand is significant. Monetization enhances your credibility, expands your reach, and generates revenue. It allows you to invest in your brand and create more value for your audience. Effective monetization ensures that your brand remains sustainable and impactful.

Managing monetization challenges involves being strategic and adaptable. Monetization can present challenges such as balancing authenticity with revenue generation and managing multiple income streams. Stay focused on your goals, seek feedback, and be willing to adjust your strategy as needed. Managing challenges ensures that your monetization efforts remain effective and aligned with your brand values.

Building a sustainable income stream involves creating diverse and reliable sources of revenue. Focus on generating passive income through digital products, affiliate marketing, and memberships. Diversify your income streams to ensure stability and sustainability. Building a sustainable income stream enhances your brand's resilience and growth.

The role of passive income in brand monetization is significant. Passive income allows you to generate revenue without continuous active effort. Focus on creating digital products, affiliate marketing, and ad revenue to build passive income streams. Passive income enhances your financial stability and provides more time to focus on creating value for your audience.

Creating value for your audience is at the heart of brand monetization. Focus on providing solutions, insights, and experiences that meet your audience's needs. Creating value enhances your credibility, attracts followers, and generates revenue. Value-driven monetization ensures that your efforts are impactful and aligned with your brand values.

Balancing monetization and authenticity is crucial. While generating revenue is important, staying true to your values and maintaining authenticity is essential. Choose monetization opportunities that align with your brand values and audience's interests. Balancing monetization and authenticity builds trust and ensures long-term success.

Legal considerations in monetization involve understanding contracts, copyright laws, and platform policies. Ensure that your monetization efforts comply with legal regulations. Understanding legal considerations protects your brand and maintains your credibility.

Measuring monetization success involves tracking metrics like revenue, conversions, and engagement. Use analytics tools to measure the performance of your monetization efforts. Regularly review these metrics to understand what's working and where you can improve. Measuring success ensures that your monetization strategy remains effective.

Leveraging technology for monetization enhances your efforts. Use tools for e-commerce, email marketing, and analytics to streamline your monetization processes. Technology ensures that your efforts are efficient and impactful. Leveraging technology enhances your ability to generate revenue and grow your brand.

Staying updated with monetization trends ensures that your strategy remains relevant and effective. Follow industry blogs, attend webinars, and participate in online courses to stay informed about the latest trends and best practices. Staying updated keeps your strategy fresh and innovative.

The future of brand monetization offers exciting opportunities. With new technologies, platforms, and strategies emerging, staying updated is crucial. Embrace new opportunities to enhance your monetization efforts. The future of brand monetization is dynamic and evolving, offering endless opportunities for growth and success.

Celebrating monetization milestones is important. Acknowledge and celebrate the revenue targets, new products, and successful partnerships. Celebrating milestones builds motivation and reinforces your commitment to achieving your monetization goals.

Now that we've explored the strategies for effective brand monetization, let's dive into the importance of continuous improvement and growth. Continuous improvement ensures that your personal branding efforts remain effective, relevant, and impactful. Let's explore how to embrace continuous improvement and achieve long-term success.

Chapter 10: Continuous Improvement and Growth

Continuous improvement and growth are like nurturing a plant. They require regular attention, care, and effort to flourish. The importance of continuous improvement in personal branding cannot be overstated. It ensures that your efforts remain effective, relevant, and impactful. Setting long-term goals provides direction and motivation. Your goals should reflect your aspirations and guide your branding efforts. Regularly review and update your goals to ensure that they remain aligned with your values and vision.

Staying updated with industry trends and best practices is essential for continuous improvement. The world is constantly changing, and staying informed helps you adapt and leverage new opportunities. Follow industry blogs, attend conferences, and participate in online courses to stay current with the latest trends and innovations.

Learning from feedback is a powerful way to improve. Seek feedback from your audience, peers, and mentors. Listen to their insights and use them to refine your strategy. Feedback provides valuable perspectives and helps you identify areas for improvement. Embrace feedback as an opportunity to learn and grow.

Adapting to changes ensures that your personal branding efforts remain relevant and effective. The digital landscape is dynamic, and being adaptable allows you to stay ahead of the curve. Embrace new technologies, platforms, and trends to keep your strategy fresh and innovative. Adapting to changes enhances your ability to connect with your audience and achieve your goals.

Building a growth mindset involves believing that your abilities and intelligence can be developed through hard work and dedication. A growth mindset embraces challenges, learns from failures, and continuously seeks improvement. Cultivate a growth mindset to stay motivated and resilient on your branding journey.

Leveraging personal development resources provides valuable opportunities for learning and growth. Use online courses, books, and workshops to enhance your skills and knowledge. Regularly invest in your personal development to stay updated and relevant. Personal development resources provide the tools and insights needed for continuous improvement.

The role of mentorship in continuous improvement is significant. Mentors provide guidance, support, and valuable insights. Seek out mentors who have successfully built their personal brands and learn from their experiences. Mentors can offer advice, introduce you to new opportunities, and help you navigate challenges.

Participating in professional development enhances your skills and knowledge. Professional development can include certifications, workshops, and conferences. Regularly invest in your professional development to stay updated and enhance your expertise. Professional development ensures that your skills remain relevant and competitive.

Networking for growth involves connecting with individuals who can support and inspire your journey. Build relationships with industry leaders, peers, and potential collaborators. Networking provides valuable insights, support, and opportunities for collaboration. It enhances your ability to achieve your long-term goals.

Staying inspired and motivated is crucial for continuous improvement. Regularly seek out new ideas, trends, and sources of inspiration. Attend conferences, read industry blogs, and connect with other content creators. Staying inspired keeps your efforts fresh and engaging. It ensures that you continue to provide value to your audience.

Embracing new opportunities involves being open to change and willing to take risks. New opportunities can include collaborations, projects, and learning experiences. Embrace opportunities that align with your values and goals. Being open to new opportunities enhances your growth and expands your reach.

The impact of continuous learning on personal branding is significant. Continuous learning keeps your skills and knowledge updated. It allows you to stay relevant and competitive. Regularly invest in your learning to stay informed and enhance your expertise. Continuous learning ensures that your branding efforts remain effective and impactful.

Measuring your progress involves tracking metrics and reviewing your efforts. Use analytics tools to measure the performance of your content, engagement, and monetization efforts. Regularly review these metrics to understand what's working and where you can improve. Measuring progress ensures that your strategy remains effective and aligned with your goals.

Overcoming growth challenges involves being persistent and creative. Growth can present challenges such as staying motivated, managing multiple tasks, and dealing with setbacks. Stay focused on your goals, seek support, and be willing to adjust your strategy as needed. Overcoming challenges ensures that you continue to grow and achieve your goals.

Celebrating small wins is important for maintaining motivation and momentum. Acknowledge and celebrate the progress and achievements, no matter how small. Celebrating small wins builds motivation and reinforces your commitment to achieving your long-term goals.

Staying resilient involves being able to bounce back from setbacks and challenges. Resilience is built through persistence, adaptability, and a positive mindset. Embrace challenges as opportunities to learn and grow. Staying resilient ensures that you can navigate obstacles and continue on your branding journey.

The role of innovation in continuous improvement is significant. Innovation involves finding new and creative ways to achieve your goals. Regularly seek out new ideas, trends, and technologies to enhance your strategy. Innovation keeps your efforts fresh and engaging. It ensures that you remain competitive and relevant.

Building a support system involves connecting with individuals who can provide encouragement, advice, and support. Your support system can include mentors, peers, friends, and family. Building a support system enhances your ability to achieve your goals and navigate challenges. It provides a network of individuals who support and promote your growth.

Leveraging technology for growth enhances your efforts. Use tools for content creation, analytics, and networking to streamline your processes and enhance your impact. Technology provides valuable resources and opportunities for innovation. Leveraging technology ensures that your branding efforts remain effective and efficient.

The importance of self-care cannot be overstated. Self-care involves taking time to rest, relax, and recharge. It ensures that you remain healthy and motivated. Regularly practice self-care to avoid burnout and maintain a positive mindset. Self-care enhances your ability to achieve your goals and maintain a sustainable branding strategy.

Managing stress and burnout is crucial for long-term success. Stress and burnout can impact your motivation and productivity. Use strategies like time management, delegation, and self-care to manage stress. Managing stress and burnout ensures that you can maintain an active and engaging presence.

The role of reflection in continuous improvement is significant. Reflection involves taking time to review your experiences, decisions, and progress. Regularly reflect on your efforts to gain valuable insights and identify areas for improvement. Reflection enhances your ability to learn and grow.

Building a legacy involves creating a lasting impact through your personal brand. Your legacy is the positive influence and contributions you make to your field and community. Focus on creating value, building relationships, and making a positive impact. Building a legacy ensures that your branding efforts have a lasting and meaningful influence.

Staying true to your values ensures that your branding efforts remain authentic and aligned with your beliefs. Your values guide your decisions and actions. Regularly review your values and ensure that they are reflected in your strategy. Staying true to your values builds trust and enhances your credibility.

The future of personal branding offers exciting opportunities. With new technologies, platforms, and strategies emerging, staying updated is crucial. Embrace new opportunities to enhance your branding efforts. The future of personal branding is dynamic and evolving, offering endless opportunities for growth and success.

The impact of personal growth on your brand is significant. Personal growth enhances your skills, knowledge, and confidence. It allows you to provide more value to your audience and achieve your goals. Regularly invest in your personal growth to stay updated and relevant. Personal growth ensures that your branding efforts remain effective and impactful.

Staying passionate and driven is crucial for long-term success. Passion is the fuel that drives you and keeps you motivated. Regularly seek out new opportunities, challenges, and sources of inspiration to stay passionate about your journey. Staying passionate ensures that you remain motivated and resilient.

Celebrating your journey involves acknowledging and appreciating your progress, achievements, and growth. Celebrate the milestones, big and small, and take pride in your accomplishments. Celebrating your journey builds motivation and reinforces your commitment to achieving your goals.

Looking ahead to new horizons involves being open to new opportunities, challenges, and growth. The journey of personal branding is continuous, offering endless opportunities for learning, growth, and success. Embrace the future with optimism and excitement, knowing that your efforts will lead to incredible opportunities and achievements.

As we conclude this comprehensive guide on personal branding, remember that building your professional identity online is a continuous journey. It requires dedication, effort, and a commitment to growth. Embrace the strategies, best practices, and insights shared in this guide to create a powerful and impactful personal brand. Your journey of personal branding is uniquely yours, filled with opportunities for growth, success, and lasting impact.

www.ingramcontent.com/pod-product-compliance
Lightning Source LLC
Chambersburg PA
CBHW072018230526
45479CB00008B/273